THIRTY DAYS *of* EXPLOSIVE PRAYERS

Darlene Hunter Fant

AuthorHouse™
1663 Liberty Drive
Bloomington, IN 47403
www.authorhouse.com
Phone: 1 (800) 839-8640

Published by AuthorHouse 04/03/2018

ISBN: 978-1-5462-3368-8 (sc)
ISBN: 978-1-5462-3367-1 (e)

Library of Congress Control Number: 2018903871

Print information available on the last page.

authorHOUSE®

THIRTY DAYS OF
EXPLOSIVE PRAYERS

BY

DARLENE HUNTER FANT

This book is dedicated to my deceased parents Anna Delgado Hunter and Jerome Hunter. And lastly to my dearest sister Regina Hunter.

FOREWORD

This book is a compilation of prayers and breathed on and inspired by the Ruach Hakadesh. I knew that when I was down an anointed prayer always lifted my burdens. I always felt much needed peace after communing with God. I got filled with the Holy Ghost when someone prayed for me, my body has been healed as well as my mind. My children were also healed.

Sometimes we get to a place in our lives that we get so overwhelmed that it is hard to utter a word. That is when an intercessor comes along to stand in the gap and pray.

The purpose of this book is to jumpstart your day and shift the atmosphere to that you feel the unction to go to the father for yourself, to bask in his presence and loving arms. To jump up on his lap, relax and tell him your problems. It is my sincere prayer that this book accomplishes just that.

If you have never asked Jesus into your life why don't you take a moment to invite Him in?

Him to forgive you of your sins. Won't you confess that He died and rose and is coming back again.

Ask Him to be head of your life. If you believe that in your heart and confess it with your mouth, YOU ARE SAVED!

Your name will be put in the Lamb's Book of Life.

Welcome to the Family!

Peace and Many Blessings

Apostle Darlene

ACKNOWLEDGEMENTS

I would like to thank my Lord and Savior Jesus Christ for introducing me to His Father Abba and to the Holy Spirit for inspiring every prayer.

To my mentor and overseer Bishop Norman H. Lyons, II for his godly guidance, patience, and nurturing.

To my children Emmanuel, Joi, Chadira, Hope, Joshua, and Caleb for their unconditional love.

To my godson Jonathan Stubberfield who always holds me down.

To the late Apostle, John H. Boyd who taught me to love, fast, and pray.

To Dubina Boyd Jones, his daughter who has never changed. Always a sister and a friend.

To Divine Destiny International Prayer Alliance (D.D.I.P.A) for their support and encouragement.

To my Sister Elder Rose Joyner

To my Armorbearer Sister Regina Laviolette

To my daughter Apostle Queena Gregory

To my spiritual sons and daughters all around the world too numerous to mention. I absolutely love, love, love you!

And to my Sister Evangelist Annette Meyers who typed the manuscript of this book with love and professionalism.

DAY 1

Lord thank you that you hold our hand in your prayerful hand. Thank you that you never let go. You never leave us or forsake us. You are a constant in our life. When my mother and father forsake me, then you will take me up! I am so grateful for your never-ending presence.

I love you and need you to lead and guide me into all truth today. You are my friend and forever companion. Let not your spirit leave me. I as this in the name of Jesus. In your name I pray and I consider it done.

DAY 2

Holy Spirit lead me and guide me today in all truth. Have your way today. Fill me to overflowing. Enlarge my capacity to house you. Take out everything that clutters and impedes you from flowing through me. I want to be a vessel and container of your power. I want to be an expression of you love today. You are everything I desire to be. Take of every hindrance that keeps me from walking in your newness. Baptize me to overflowing. Let your consuming fire burn out the dross. Let your consuming fire burn out the sin and every weight that besets me fill me until I sing in another language, pray in another language, dance and move in you. Thank you I pray in Jesus' name

Amen

DAY 3

Sweep over me Holy Spirit. Sweep over me spirit of the living God. Refresh me with your presence, transform me like only you can, for your glory. Touch me with your fingers of love turn me towards the things of God. Move me away from the things of this world. I desire more of you. I don't even want the hint or the smell of this world. I belong to a new kingdom. I am a citizen of a better world. Help me to represent your kingdom today on the earth. Let the fragrance of the kingdom be lingering on me and every place my foot treads today. Let the atmosphere shift because I allow your Spirit to endue me with power that causes change. I thank you for using me today. It's in the name of Jesus I pray………. AMEN

DAY 4

Dear Lord I believe everything and every word that proceeds out of the mouth of the Lord. I stand and walk in faith today. I have a made-up mind. I have my face set like a flint. I shall not be moved by what I hear or see. I shall only be moved by what I hear the Holy Spirit speak. He shows me Jesus. He leads and guides me into all truth. Let your truth abide in me today. Let me speak with authority and abundant power. Let me use my voice to create change on this earth. Thank you for the awesome privilege to be used by you. This day someone will come to know you better because I yielded to you. I ask this in the name of Jesus the Christ I pray....... Amen

DAY 5

Lord I bare my soul to you today. Let me be transparent before you. Help me to hold nothing back. Search the depths of my heart. Go into those places I have kept hidden even from you. Sweep them clean. Purge me with your blood. Cleanse me from secret faults. Make me whole. I desire to exhibit your fruits today. Love, kindness, peace, joy, gentleness, temperance and longsuffering.

Let someone know that the secret to your ever-flowing spirit is being yielded to you. Trusting you. Leaning and depending on you. Eating your word. Immersed in your spirit today. That is my goal and prayer. Take all of me oh Lord. Mold me, shape me and fashion me in your image I pray!

Amen

DAY 6

Father I thank you for this day. I thank you that you will speak to my heart today. That you will show me the things to come upon the earth and in my life. Help me to open my mind to the supernatural realm that I would walk in heavenly places with you. You said we are seated in heavenly places with you. Let me see things from that vantage point today. Not looking down, but looking up remember who I am in you.

I love you and thank you. Teach me how to see things the way you do! With all my getting, let me get an understanding in the Name of Jesus I pray…. Amen

DAY 7

Father God in the Name of Jesus, I give you this day. Hold me, make me, shape me in your ways, oh Lord. Give me your understanding in everything I do today. You said if I acknowledge you in all my ways, you would direct my path. Please order my steps and my conversation a right today. I want to speak your words. I want to use my tongue to bring forth the things you want done on this earth. I desire to be a conduit between heaven and earth. I desire to show forth your praise and glory this day through me your servant.

It's in the name of Jesus I pray…. Amen

DAY 8

Our father and our God in the Name of Jesus I come to you as humbly as I know how. I acknowledge that I transgressed against you and you alone. I desire to be a vessel of honor set apart for your use. I don't understand everything but this I know, I know without you I'm nothing and I can do nothing. Please mold me and fashion me in your likeness. I want to see you when I look in the mirror. A reflection of your love and an extension of your power. I give this day back to you to have your way and your will. I ask all these things in the Name of Jesus and I call them done…. Amen

DAY 9

Our Father and our God in the Name of Jesus. We worship you in the beauty of holiness. You said, "Be ye holy, for I am holy. Take off everything that hinders me and keeps me from being all I can be in you. Take my heart and cleanse my lips. Purify my thoughts, order my steps, renew and revive the covenant we have made. Remind me of the things I have failed to do that I promised you. Give me another chance to get it right. I desire to hold up my part of the covenant. Thank you, this day. A new day that you can write on me. I am an empty canvas. Do with me as you will. It's in the Name of Jesus I pray and count if done…. Amen

Day 10

Oh Lord, I give you thanks for this day! You and you alone have been my refuge and my fortress. A safe place, my refuge in the time of storm.

Turmoil and pain have surrounded me. But you encompassed me as with a shield. You are my armor, my buckler, my protector, and soon coming King. I extol you. I magnify you. I bow down before you. I worship at your feet. I am humbled by your magnificence. I am overwhelmed by your presence.

Who can stand before you? Loving you is better than life. I desire to know you better, in the power of your resurrection and in the fellowship of your sufferings. I am in awe of you.

Thank you for saving me. It is in the name of Jesus I pray......Amen

DAY 11

Dear Lord please have mercy on our millenniums. This generation is so inundated evil and wrong messages. They are hearing that an abortion is okay. Being gay is okay. Get what you want even if you must rob and steal. There are no absolutes. They are confused and hurting. Oh Lord, please intervene and take the veil off their eyes. Please lead them and guide them and guide them into all truth. Please surround them as with a shield.

We bless them, we pray for them. We declare they shall not be a lost generation, but strong witness for you!

We as this in the Name of Yeshua Hamashiach and we call it done.

Day 12

Dear God, we worship you in the beauty of holiness. We life your name on high. You are altogether lovely. You are everything we could every need and more. Nobody nowhere like you.

We love you this day. Have you way oh Lord! Not my will, but thy will be done today and every day.

I have tried it my Lord. That way has led to destruction. You told us to acknowledge you in all our ways and you would direct our paths.

Please lead me today, guide me with your watchful eye.

I am so grateful that you are my heavenly father. My leader, guide and protector. Have your way this and forever. In Jesus Name I pray…. Amen

Day 13

Dear Father and our God in the name of Jesus we come first just saying thank you. Thank you for grace and loving kindness. It is to you and you alone that I look. My gaze is upwards. I look to the hills from whence cometh my help. My help cometh from you oh Lord! You are my help in the time of trouble. You are my buckler and my shield, my all sufficiency, my everything. Nothing compares to you. All the silver and gold dulls in comparison to your light. You are the epitome of everything that is good. I am so glad you are my father and I am your child. Let nothing ever come between me and thee!

It's in the Name of Jesus I pray…..Amen

Day 14

I will bless the Lord always. His praise shall continually be in my mouth.

This is the day I purpose in my mind to praise and not complain. To shout and not pout. To raise my hands in surrender to all your ways. You are my guide. In you I live and move and have my being. I desire to be a channel of your love and a vessel of honor. I esteem your words and well higher than my necessary food. I realize the thing that I see are temporary, but the things I don't see are eternal. Only what I do for you will matter in eternity. Help me to see past this natural world. To put on my spiritual eyes so I can see things the way you do. I bless your holy name and love you so very much. It in the Name of Jesus I pray....Amen

DAY 15

Lord I need thee. You are my help. You are my deliverer and you are my soon coming King. I have found I can do nothing without you. But I can do all things through you who strengthens me.

Today it seems as if I am troubled on every side. But I know that if you are with me, you are more than the world against me. I know you said, "Many are the afflictions of the righteous, but you promise to deliver us out of them all." Let God arise and His enemies be scattered.

Today I speak to every demonic force that tries to take my peace, my joy, and my faith. You said we have authority over all the power of the enemy. I will walk on my high places today. Make my feet like hind's feet. Make my face like a flint. Teach my hands to fight and my fingers to war.

Oh, how I need thee. Every hour I need thee.

So glad you never leave me nor forsake me.

I love you Jesus. Thank you for your loving kindness and great grace.

I ask all these things in the Name of Jesus the Christ, and consider them done!

Amen

Day 16

Heavenly Father I come to you on bended knees and a humble heart. I ask that you remove anything from me that displeases you. I desire to be a vessel honor fit for the Master's use.

I repent of unbelief, procrastination, slothfulness and complaining.

Lord help my unbelief. I want to trust you with my whole heart. To believe in your finished work on the cross. Knowing that every prayer, every request, every work was wrought at Calvary. You completed your course. Help me to do the same. to run this race with patience that has been set before me. I endeavor to finish my course to complete my assignment that you have given me.

Help me to please you in everything I say and do. I ask this humbly in the Name of Jesus the Christ I pray…. Amen

Day 17

Lord I thank you for the things you are accomplishing in me as I go through this wilderness experience. I thank you for your spirit that leads me and guides me on this journey.

I feel so weary and thirsty, but I know you are my strength. You are water in the desert places and a fountain to my soul.

You have made some promises that seem so far off. But I know a day with you is as a thousand years. But I also know you have given me the vision and it shall come to pass.

Help me to hold on as I grope in the darkness and traverse unknown territory. Extend your great hands towards me. Hold me up as I feel faint. Change my mind as I want to look back. Help me to walk upright through life. You said, no good thing will I withhold from them that walk uprightly. I shall wait until my change comes. I shall trust you until I see the vision manifested in the natural.

Thank you for infusing me with strength to hold on to you unchanging hands.

I bless your Holy Name!

Amen

Day 18

Our Father and our God all of creation is waiting for return.

Lord when will you return? Your children are ready to go home.

We miss being in your presence continually. We are thankful for the visitations, but we desire to live and abide with you eternally.

This world is not our home. We know you went to prepare a place for us.

Come quickly Lord Jesus! Your children need you.

Evil has become the way of the world. It's a chaotic place. Thank you for your peace that surpasses all understanding. Your grace has been sufficient, but our soul longs for you so much more.

You are our desire. Our souls long and pant for you. Thank you for hearing this prayer. Help us to stay the course as we await your glorious appearing.

We ask this in the Name of Jesus the Christ we pray!

Amen

Day 19

My how the enemy has risen against us! We are grateful that you are our shield and buckler. Avery present help in the time of need.

When our heart is overwhelmed we can run boldly to the throne of grace to obtain help in the time of need.

You have been our refuge and our fortress. You have hidden us under the shadow of your wings.

You have been that rock that is higher than I.

Thank God for your many mercies and kindness. What would we do without you? Where would we go?

Your grace has been sufficient. Your love overwhelms me. I am grateful to be your child

In your presence I find love, joy, and peace.

Please never take your spirit away from me or cast me from your presence.

I pray this prayer in your name. In the name of Jesus, Yeshua Hamashiach I pray…. Amen

Day 20

In your presence that is where I belong. In your presence, oh Lord my God is where I long to be.

Our father and our God in the name of Jesus. We come first just to say thank you.

We thank you for your unfailing love. Your grace has been sufficient.

Your love has been water in a desert place. Your mercy has been more than I deserve.

I want to thank you for how you take loving care of me. How you never leave me nor forsake me. How you keep me close so that I don't fall.

Thank you, sweet Jesus. You are a good good Father. You are a shelter in the rain. An ever-present help in the time of trouble. My soul longs for your appearing, for the day I shall behold you face to face.

Thank you for undergirding me and keeping my steps from failing. I would have fainted except like David I believe to see the goodness of the Lord in the land of the living.

Thank you for my hope that lies in you.

I ask this in Jesus' name and I consider it done!

Day 21

My soul thirsts for you oh Lord. You're the only one that quenches my dry life. Your water to the thirsty and bread to the hungry. You are my all sufficiency. When my mother and my father forsake me, then you shall take me up. You lift me high above my enemies. High above my trials, tribulation, and pain.

You are the glory and the lifter of my head. You make my crooked places straight and my rough places smooth. You make your light to shine in my dark places.

You are a light in my dark world. You are the way in a twisted, evil land. I love that I can walk in your presence. In the anointing I can breathe. I can think clearly. I can walk on my high places. I can be free.

Thank you for the fresh wind of the Holy Ghost that blows gently on my face. Awakening the dead parts of me. Thank you for your constant love and compassion.

Thank you, Jesus, for all you are to me and to all the world…..Amen

Day 22

Lord I thank you that my days are numbered and that you hold my life in your hands. You have a book that tells of the things you have planned for me. You have plan for my life. It is a plan of good and not evil. I pray that I fulfill all you have written for me. That I fulfill my assignment. I thank you for the cloud of witnesses that have gone before me, cheering me on. You are a God of order. You completed everything you came to do. Help me to the same. I want you to be pleased when I get to heaven. I don't want anything to be left undone. You died on a rugged cross that I might have abundant life and power from on high.

Your dunamis propels me to higher heights. Please strive with me always. I need you more than my necessary food. I need to know that no matter where this life takes me, that you are already there. Love you Jesus…..Amen

Day 23

Lord I thank you because you have been my protector you have hidden me beneath your wings.

When my enemies and my foes came upon me to eat up my flesh they stumbled and fell. I love you because when no else cares you are there. You told me to cast my cares upon you because you care for me. You take my pain and turn it into strength. You take my sorrow and turn it into joy. You are my joy and peace and my reason for living.

Once I was blind and now I see. Once I was lost but now I'm found. You took me out of a dark place and brought me into your Kingdom of Light.

I so love you Jesus. Where would I be if it had not been for you who was on my side? Day by day I give thanks that you are my Father and the keeper of my soul.

DAY 24

Father God in the Name of Jesus, I stand before you knowing I can do NOTHING without you, but that I can do ALL things because of you. The pain and darkness I see around me tries to confuse me and keep me in bondage. And then I remember that you came to give me life and that more abundantly. The entrance of your word gives light. Light my path on today. Renew my strength. Restore my resolve until I become saturated in the anointing that destroys yokes. Make me a beacon of light and hope in this sin sick world use me to change and shift the atmosphere of the hopelessness to one of power and change and strength. This is my prayer I ask in the Name of Jesus and count it done…. Amen

DAY 25

As the deer pants for the water, so do I pant after you oh Lord. Thank you that you have introduced me to your Father Jehovah. That the same way I have pursued you that there is now a thirst to get to know the Father. He has remained a mystery but you have been the door that has led to my relationship with Him. How I hunger to know and love Him more. What a privilege to be able to go to the throne of grace and obtain help in the time of need. He has been our ALL SUFFICIENCY. Imagine having an audience with the I AM THAT I AM. EVERYTHING WE EVER NEEDED AND SO MUCH MORE! Thank you, dear Jesus, that you would show us the Father!

DAY 26

Lord give me the tongue of the pen of a ready writer. Help me to pray and sing love songs into you today. I pray as I sing and wait on you that you will reveal your glory in my life and in the lives of those who I am connected to. Help me to seek your face and your direction today. Help me to keep first things first. You and your needs before mine. Let this day pattern what you have planned what you planned for me. Not my will, but thy will be done on today. Shape me into who you have desire before the foundation of the word. Mold me, shape me, use me. Use this tongue to create an atmosphere that welcomes your presence. On how I love you! Thank you for this day! I shall rejoice and be glad in it!

DAY 27

Father as I wait in your presence I feel your strength you said that they that wait upon the Lord shall renew their strength. Help me to mount up in my most holy faith. The enemy of my soul tries to keep me laden down with burdens. But as I wait in your presence, I realize that you are a burden bearer. You admonish us to cast our care on you, because you care for us. Sometimes it's hard to let go and allow you and unite you into the deepest darkest parts of me. I know you understand and desire to help. But sometimes I feel like I can handle certain things on my own. But the more I am around you the more I stay in your presence. I realize that I need you. I realize that it is your good pleasure to take every burden and every hurt from your children. You desire to wrap us up in your eternal blanket of love and understanding. We are your heart and you have become my heartbeat. We are now being as one. I am really learning what it means to lean completely on you and allow you to make me complete in you. Thank you for your patience and loving kindness.

I ask this in your name, that name that changes things. It is in Jesus', Your Name I pray!

Amen

DAY 28

Lord help me to do things the way you do them. While you walked the earth, you said that you do the things that you see the Father do. Help me to pattern that behavior. Help me to do the things you do and in the way, you do them. I want to reflect your power in this earth. An expression of your love. You love my enemies and those that hurt and persecute us because of you. You said that great was our reward. I desire to love, pray, and bless them that hurt me. And to forgive them and trust you to undergird me. Your ways are not my ways your thoughts are not my thoughts. They are as far as the heaven is from the ear. I see I have made strides, but have so far to go. Help me oh Lord to reach my goal. I don't want to keep missing the mark. Anoint me to do what I see you do. I ask this in the Name of Jesus and call it done…. Amen

DAY 29

Lord you said that you would shake the nations. Please shake this nation, the greatest nation on earth. We were established in Judeo-Christian principles. We have gone so far away from the foundations that were birthed. Help us to return to our first love. We prayed for children in school, we found homes for children that had nowhere to go. We did not abort them. We respected authority. We loved our neighbors. Oh Lord bring us back to the Old Landmark. We've strayed so far from where we have begun. We are paying the price. We have become so politically correct we no longer have compassion as to what is right and what is wrong. We need you to pray for our nation that we would lead a peaceable life we pray and interceded for this nation that it would be great again what we would go to our houses of worship that we would worship together in our homes, our schools, our places of employment. That you would be high and lifted in this nation again. That we would care for one another especially the least among us.

This is my prayer and I know that you hear me because I have asked in faith.

Amen

DAY 30

What can we say to these things? What can separate us from the love of God in Christ Jesus?

Lord I've purposed in my heart NOT to allow anyone or anything to separate me from you. You have been my dwelling place, my strong tower, my deliverer. You have been my all sufficiency. Without you I just could not go on. People have come and people have gone. Many have made many promises and didn't keep or honor them. But you and you alone have been there through it all.

You have put your hand over me and covered me. Your hand has healed, sustained, and saved me. Your voice has been a lighthouse in the times of storm. You Word has been a lamp unto my feet and a light unto my path. Your love has surrounded me and carried me through this complicated existence called life.

I love, honor, and adore you. I pray that these prayers that you have prayed through me strengthens and encourages someone else to run this race with patience and courage.

I thank you for choosing me to be a beacon of light and love in this day and hour.

Please bless all that read this book with joy, hope and stamina. Teach us to endure hardness as a good soldier and outlast the enemy. Help us to run on to our wealthy place. To that place called THERE that flows with milk and honey.

Thank you, father, for who you are and what you do.

It is in the Name of Jesus we pray and call it done!

Amen

ABOUT THE AUTHOR

Darlene Hunter Fant

Darlene is an Apostle whose ministry was birthed under Norman H. Lyons, II, Apostle and Senior Pastor of the Fountain of Life Church in Uniondale, New York. She has been preaching and teaching for over 20 years. She is the visionary and Apostolic mentor at Divine Destiny International Prayer Alliance (D.D.I.P.A.) which meets online, through teleconferencing, Facebook Live, and has annual conferences and gatherings in cities throughout the United States.

Divine Destiny International Prayer Alliance has approximately 1000 intercessors and churches and ministries around the world under her covering.

Darlene Hunter Fant is the mother of six children and too many spiritual children to number. This is her first book with another book detailing her life to follow. The Late Apostle John H. Boyd, Sr. was her spiritual father, mentor, and hero.

CPSIA information can be obtained
at www.ICGtesting.com
Printed in the USA
LVHW07s0900210518
577925LV00017B/305/P

9 781546 233688